NEIL KENNEDY

Bedding Ishtar

First edition

This book was professionally typeset on Reedsy.
Find out more at reedsy.com

Contents

1

The Precious Life of Man

> ***For on account of a harlot, a man is brought to a piece of bread, and the adulteress stalks* and snares *[as with a hook] the precious life [of a man]. - Solomon (Proverbs 6:26, Amplified Classic Edition)***

I've seen it. You've seen it. The sad depreciation of a man's precious life.

For what?

For a few minutes with a harlot—whether physically or by looking at porn. Either carry the gravitational weight of failure. Guilt. Shame. Even, perhaps, suicidal thoughts.

What was so alluring that a man would risk it all?

His relationship with God. His wife. His children. His reputation, career, money, and integrity. Everything he had dreamed of and worked so hard for—for what?

Most quickly dismiss such a man as a flawed character, lacking judgment, undisciplined, or just stupid. Others pile on questions about his integrity. The murmuring, the whispering and judging, ridicule and mockery follow him. He becomes a joke. Laughing fodder. His manhood is reduced to a hypocritical caricature of toxic masculinity.

Friends and brothers distance themselves so as not to be associated with the fallen, lest they are perceived as complicit in his moral sin. He becomes a spiritual leper—keep your distance or you may be tainted.

Before we judge him too quickly we should try to understand what kind of man would succumb to such a temptation. It would be easy to think that only weak men with flawed characters would be susceptible. That would be incorrect.

> ***For she hath cast down many wounded: yea, many strong men have been slain by her. —Proverbs 7:26***

Proverbs tells us that she—The Harlot—has slain strong men. It's not just the wounded she hunts, she goes after trophies. She wants to conquer the strong man.

I've known men who desired God, men who loved their wives and adored their children, fall into her seductive arms. Somehow, these men were enticed by her—The Harlot.

Very much like Samson in the Bible, who was an incredibly

strong man, both physically and mentally. He was so smart that he played the game of riddles with his opponents. He was also anointed and supernaturally empowered by God as well.

Samson was a very strong man with a very weak resistance for the Prostitute.

Or how about David? David is described as a man after God's own heart. Yet, he too was captivated by the lure of a bathing woman.

> ***For David had done what was right in the eyes of the Lord and had not failed to keep any of the Lord's commands all the days of his life—except in the case of Uriah the Hittite. —1 Kings 15:5 (New International Version)***

David was a strong man. A warrior. A king. Yet, there's the footnote, ***"except in the case of Uriah the Hittite."*** This reference to David's adultery and murder of Uriah, although forgiven, cost David a tremendous toll.

So yes, I've seen good men, strong men, get ensnared by The Harlot. And to be sure, she attracts the wounded as well. Even easier prey.

The wounded man's pursuit of her may be sparked by childhood trauma, abuse, or molestation. He may be appeasing a father wound. Or, as I have discovered by speaking with men, intimacies with their wives are few and far between.

> **Strong or weak. It makes no difference. All men are susceptible to the wiles of The Harlot.**

The collateral damage is immeasurable. Everything a man has ever done up to that moment is scrap-heaped on his failure. It will be almost impossible for the fallen to regain respect. His influence will always be marked with the footnote of his sad downfall.

Reduced to Bread

It's a pretty graphic description that when a man joins himself with a harlot, he is reduced to a piece of bread. His life seems valueless in the aftermath.

I have wept many times with men who have faced the downfall of sexual sin. Not once did I feel superior to them. Actually, the opposite. I knew these men were just like me, trying to live their lives in faithfulness, integrity, and honor toward God, their wives, and their children. Each time it happens, I call them. I text them. I encourage them. I do whatever I can to help them navigate the reclaiming of their lives.

These encounters made me realize there is something extremely powerful involved in the take down of these men. Something so much more than flawed character, lack of intellect, or undisciplined behavior.

These fallen men were involved in an epic battle — a spiritual battle they may have been unprepared for, ignorant of their opponent, deceived to think their secret vice could be "managed" rather than conquered.

I have waited twelve years to write this book.

Had I written this book too early, I may have addressed it as so many others have. I may have attempted to write a motivational book for men urging them to discipline themselves to holiness. It would have failed to help anyone. It would have been a disservice.

I may have talked men into joining a support group and "finding someone to hold them accountable." This too would have been very disappointing because it simply does not work. (I will deal with the failure of the "accountability" message later in this book.)

Men need more than discipline. Men require deliverance.

First, let's get to the bottom of why The Harlot is such an aggressive and powerful force of destruction in men's lives.

> ***For we do not wrestle against flesh and blood, but against the rulers, against the authorities, against the cosmic powers over this present darkness, against the spiritual forces of evil in the heavenly places. — Ephesians 6:12 (English Standard Version)***

Wars are fought in the heavens before victories are realized on

Earth.

Men, you must realize that you are not in a flesh and blood battle. This means you will not win this in your own strength. You're facing rulers, authorities, cosmic powers over darkness, and against spiritual forces of evil.

Later, as we gain an understanding of this spiritual battle, I will give you the keys to align your heart so you can have victory over The Harlot.

The Harlot

The word harlot in Hebrew is *zānâ*, which means to "*go whoring after.*" The term is not limited to the physical act of adultery or sexual sin; it indicates a deeper, more sinister sin of idolatry — communing and intimacies with spirits.

> **What we do physically affects us spiritually. Likewise, what we do spiritually affects us physically.**

The physical act of adultery is the joining of a male and female in a sexual act. However, as we all know, there is much more going on than the fleshly act of a sexual relationship.

In the sexual act, two people become one in flesh. It's more than just sex. It is a design of completion. A type of communion. It is certainly a covenant.

In the design of mankind, God created a complementary form so that the male and female perfectly fit and have the function to procreate after their own kind. Sex is designed to fulfill our created purpose, namely being fruitful and multiplying on the Earth. To motivate us to fulfill our purpose, we have sexual appetites. The craving for copulating causes us to pursue one another. This comes with the rewards of passions — love, companionship, security, respect, honor, and integrity. All of these passions are secured in a covenant of marriage. The two become one.

Remember, God said that we would multiply. It is not addition, but multiplication. The sum of one plus one equals two; however, one multiplied by one equals one. The result of this multiplier blessing is producing the reflective image of God, after our own kind.

Sex is designed for consummating a marriage covenant.

The physical consummates the spiritual. In the case of marriage, the covenant is not binding until the consummation. Covenant is the idea of cutting and shedding blood. Figuratively, it is the male cutting with his knife a woman's hymen proving purity with the issue of blood on a testimonial cloth or proof of virginity cloth (see Deuteronomy 22:13-21).

The joining of a man and woman sexually was and is a big deal! In our lifetime, the devaluing of marriage has caused immeasurable harm to our society. This is how a society commits suicide.

Sexual relations have become so devalued as to be considered merely "friends with benefits." The intimacy of copulation is no longer shared by two people in love. They are merely servicing one another for impure carnal lusts.

Regardless of how society has moved the ancient boundary stones of marriage, it is far from trivial. As men, we do not get to rewrite the rules that God has established. He set up the system to work perfectly. If we live accordingly, we're blessed. If we break the rules, we're cursed.

> ***And don't you realize that if a man joins himself to a prostitute, he becomes one body with her? For the Scriptures say, "The two are united into one."—1 Corinthians 6:16 (New Living Translation)***

Paul is appalled that men of God, followers of Christ, and Temples of the Holy Spirit, would unite themselves with a prostitute.

Paul understands what is happening spiritually!

When a Believer, filled with the Holy Spirit, unites himself with a prostitute, he is in effect mingling the Holy with the profane. God forbid!

The Greek word prostitute is *pornē.* It is one who sells her body for gain. The gain may be financial for a woman. For the spirit guiding the woman, she gains something of more value, more precious. She gains the man's life. That being the man's power, his influence, and his standing as an authentic man. She slays him.

Obviously, *Pornē* is where we get the word for porn and pornography.

The word pornography is "*writing about prostitutes.*" Before the technological use of pictures, pornography was written or imaged in a carving of some sort. Writing about prostitution unleashed men's carnal imaginations. The word porn now includes digital images of prostitutes. Porn is the depiction of erotic behavior (as in pictures or writing) intended to cause sexual excitement.

Creating a carving of a prostitute took adultery to another dimension of fantastical imagination — it personified porn into an image. Porn became an idol.

Porn Became Idolatry

There is something more powerful and attractive behind the action of looking at pixels on the screen. What is so alluring in the images of porn that men become addicted to them? Men can't have a relationship with a pixel. There must be something else.

> What is so powerful that men will risk their marriage, their dignity, their jobs, and the respect of their

> children so that they can chase fantasies with pixels?

> ***I made a covenant with my eyes not to look lustfully at a young woman. —Job 31:1***

Job knew that his eyes would lead his heart. His behavior may have been secret but it wasn't private. He knew that looking at a young woman, undressing her in his imagination, was a violation of authentic manhood. He said, ***"If my heart has been enticed by another woman, or if I have lurked at my neighbor's door..."***

Job knew that looking at a woman lustfully would affect his heart. Notice, the member of his body affected would be his heart — the center of his being — his soul and spirit would be affected, not only by what he would do physically but even by his imagination.

> ***...if my steps have turned from the path, if my heart has been led by my eyes, or if my hands have been defiled... — Job 31:7***

Is looking at porn with your eyes the same as the physical consummation with prostitutes? Yes!

Most men don't think this way. They are deceived to think that adultery is a sin but porn is a private vice they can manage.

> ***You have heard that it was said, You shall not commit adultery. [Exodus. 20:14; Deuteronomy. 5:18.]***

> ***But I say to you that everyone who so much as looks at a woman with evil desire for her has already committed adultery with her in his heart. - Matthew 5:27-28 (Amplified Classic Version)***

Adultery becomes *idolatry* when the sexual act is imagined.

Idolatry is *teraphim* which is a type of divination. The *teraphim* is a small image that becomes a channel to spirits. Men carved their Teraphim from wood or stone. They wanted a physical image of their fantasy. In the age of technology, the Teraphim are pixels of photography. Porn becomes idolatry.

Communing with Spirits

> ***For rebellion is like the sin of divination, and arrogance like the evil of idolatry. Because you have rejected the word of the LORD, he has rejected you as king. — 1 Samuel 15:23 (New International Version)***

The Prophet Samuel addressed Saul's disobedience to follow the Word of the Lord. The consequence of Saul rejecting the Word is his rejection as king of Israel.

Although chosen to be the first king of Israel, Saul proved to lack the character for his title and the anointing that came with it. After Saul rebelled against the Word of the Lord, divination and idolatry played out in his life. The anointing on his title departed so that he no longer had Divine insight.

Can you imagine trying to lead a nation of God's people without the spiritual insight to do so? Israel was surrounded by adversaries, yet now they had a king without the anointing.

I recall speaking with a man who forfeited his life with immoral conduct. This man once led with dignity, intelligence, and spiritual insight. However, after speaking with him, he mumbled, his mind was confused, and he seemed juvenile in our conversation. I asked the more seasoned man with me, "What happened to him?"

He replied, "Neil, you've seen a man without the anointing on his life."

When facing a fight with the Philistines, Saul was terrified by fear so he sought counsel from the Lord in dreams, by the Urim (a stone for Divine guidance authorized by God), and by prophets. However, no channel of wisdom and insight was open to Saul. He had been cut off from authorized access.

In desperation, Saul asked his attendants to find him a medium, something forbidden in scripture.

> ***Let no one be found among you who sacrifices their son or daughter in the fire, who practices divination or sorcery, interprets omens, engages in witchcraft, or casts spells, or who is a medium or spiritist or who consults the dead. —Deuteronomy 18:10–11 (New International Version)***

Saul engaged a spiritual woman to practice necromancy —

consulting the dead for secret knowledge. He asks for the deceased prophet Samuel to come to him with a word from the Lord.

Necromancy has become entertainment in our culture. The obsession with Zombies is necromancy. Zombies are corpses aroused to life by witchcraft. They're not cute, funny, entertaining, or harmless. They are demonic. Playing games with them, being entertained by them, and allowing them to babysit your children are not harmless activities. You are communing with spirits.

Listen carefully, I've seen a lot of men enticed by women whom they perceived as spiritual. A woman who consults with the dead, practices divination, or is a witch is ungodly and is filled with evil spirits.

Just because a woman is spiritual doesn't mean she is godly.

When Saul rebels against the Word of the Lord, divination becomes idolatry and manifests in his life.

When a man devolves, he transfers his power in a sexual relationship, his manhood is devalued to what is the cheapest of foods—bread—the most common of foods to be eaten. When a man is reduced by sexual sin, he is the most common of men, easily devoured. He loses the prestige of his manhood. He becomes laughing chatter, a mockery of sorts.

> ***For on account of a harlot, a man is brought to a piece of bread, and the adulteress stalks*** **and snares** ***[as with***

> ***a hook] the precious life [of a man]. - Proverbs 6:26 (Amplified Classic Edition)***

It is a disgusting reduction of his authentic manhood.

I loathe what happens when a man is entrapped by sexual sin. I don't jump to judge the man; instead, I weep for him. Knowing that his manhood is now a mockery of what he wanted to be — an example of authenticity, integrity, and faithfulness toward God.

Notice in Proverbs 6, Solomon says the adulteress stalks the precious life of a man. She goes after him. She is on the hunt. For her, *he* is the sport. She entraps him in her snare. She wants the trophy on her mantle.

Who is she? Who is the adulteress? Who is this warrior woman hunting for the precious life of a man?

She is Not a Woman, She is a Spirit

This is where I want you to think very clearly. **She is not a woman**. She is a spirit that ***uses*** women. This spirit is filled with misandry — a deep contempt for manhood. She has an antipathy for manhood and will use a woman to entice a man into her snare.

I want to be very clear before I go any further. I am not attacking women.

On the contrary, as men, we should be gallant toward women.

That means we treat all women with respect and special honor. We are to treat older women as we would our mothers. We treat younger women as we would our daughters. We treat peers as we would treat our sisters. Our wives are the only women who attract our eye's intimacy and our loin's passions.

No woman will be treated better than a woman who is in a relationship with an authentic man — a FivestarMan.

I also want to make note of the millions of women who are enslaved in modern sex trafficking rings throughout the world. These women are victims. They are not prostitutes by choice. They are the victims of their perpetrators and the men who abuse them.

Porn is a sexual fantasy with the image of a prostitute.

There are women who channel the spirit of prostitution. We're not dealing with natural women, but a spirit being, a demon — we're being hunted by a seductress spirit.

Behind the image of the prostitute is a demon goddess named *Ishtar*. Her ambition is a sinister plot, which is to reduce men to be valueless in influence, impotent in authority, and cursed by the claws of her seduction. She wants men to be emasculated. She wants his power. She wants his manhood.

An ancient inscription declared,

My Ishtar, Mistress of battle and conflict, turn his masculinity into femininity.

2

Bedding Ishtar

"But I have a few complaints against you. You tolerate some among you whose teaching is like that of Balaam, who showed Balak how to trip up the people of Israel. He taught them to sin by eating food offered to idols and by committing sexual sin. - Revelation 2:14

The Sin at Acacia Grove

When Balak, the king of Moab, heard what Israel had done to his cousins, the Amorites, he was terrified. Knowing that he did not have a standing army that could defeat the Israelites, Balak sought to destroy them by divination.

> **When your enemy knows that you are a strong man, he or she will use divination, often through doctrines of demons or false prophecies to entice you. When**

> **you're blessed, you can't be cursed unless you open a gate for your enemy to access.**

Balak's only option to defeat the men of Israel was for the gods to curse them, so he paid the fee of divination to hire Balaam to work his magic.

Three times, Balaam's oracles became blessings because the Angel of the Lord repeatedly warned him to not curse the Israelites. He could not curse whom God had blessed.

> ***Like a fluttering sparrow or a darting swallow, an undeserved curse does not come to rest. — Proverbs 26:2 (New International Version)***

Remember the flaming sword of the Angel of the Lord and Balaam's donkey not obeying him? It shows how serious Yahweh was in protecting the utterances that Balaam would speak.

Since Balaam could not curse Israel, he tapped into his magic arts and taught Balak a *doctrine* on how to entice Israel to sin.

> ***The Spirit clearly says that in later times some will abandon the faith and follow deceiving spirits and things taught by demons. — 1 Timothy 4:1 (New International Version)***

Although the Angel of the Lord spoke to Balaam, he was not a prophet of Yahweh. Balaam was a heathen prophet that used divination to receive oracles.

Balaam is associated with the goddess, Ashtar, also known as Inanna or Ishtar.

> ***While the Israelites were camped at Acacia Grove, some of the men defiled themselves by having sexual relations with local Moabite women. These women invited them to attend sacrifices to their gods, so the Israelites feasted with them and worshiped the gods of Moab. In this way, Israel joined in the worship of Baal of Peor, causing the Lord's anger to blaze against his people. —Numbers 25:1–3 (New International Version)***

Descended from Incest

The Moabites were descendants of Lot, Abraham's nephew, who settled in the valley of Sodom and Gomorrah. Lot's choice of the plains proved to be a snare for him and his family. As beautiful as the plains were, the cities were populated with violent and perverse people. The atmosphere was exceptionally wicked.

> **The atmosphere you allow in your home becomes the culture of your children.**

Abraham pleaded with the justice of God to lower His requirement of righteous standing in the city down to only ten people in order to spare the judgment against Sodom and Gomorrah. Yet, not even ten righteous people could be gathered.

Only Lot and his daughters survived the fiery storm of judgment.

After the destruction of Sodom and Gomorrah, Lot's daughters feared there were no men left on Earth. They feared barrenness. So they devised a scheme to have sexual relationships with their father. Out of this incestual relationship were born the progeny of the Moabites and the Ammonites. Those born out of this perversion did not worship the God of Abraham. They associated themselves with two gods, *Chemosh* and *Ashtar-Chemosh.*

The doctrine of Balaam which enticed the sin of Israel at Acacia Grove involved sexual relationships with Moabite women, feasting on foods sacrificed to idols (a type of communion), and worshiping the goddess Ishtar.

Worship of Chemosh involved child sacrifices. The degrading of humanity is never more evident than when men and women sacrifice their children on altars of deities.

Abortion is not just an inconvenient choice for a woman but involves a much deeper and more sinister sin—infanticide. Our culture is depraved in its collective mind toward the killing of children in the sacred womb of their mothers. It is illogical to conclude that a child within the womb is of no human value. It's not rational. It is inspired by a malevolent spirit. A bloodthirsty anti-man spirit feeds on the destruction of man's progeny through abortion.

The sin at Acacia Grove is evidence of the gravitational descent of depravity.

The reference to Israel joining in the worship of Baal of Peor means they plummeted to the depravity of worshiping who we know as Baal, also known as Baʿal Zebub, lord of the flies, which is a reference to the filth of dung, and pestilence that follows him. Baal is a diseased, pestilent, filthy, dirty, disgusting, and rotting evil spirit.

(Let me pause for a minute and explain something. I am sharing this content so you receive the revelation that porn is NOT just a secret little vice that men enjoy to manage stress, deal with insecurities, desire affection, or play fantasy games. Porn is a demon spirit. When you grasp this reality you will never want to engage in this awful depravity again. This is a serious spiritual battle. If you'll continue reading, I will show you how to defeat this demon and win this spiritual battle.)

Ashtar-Chemosh (Ishtar-Che mosh) is the goddess of prostitution.

Who is Ishtar?

Ishtar is called the Lady of Heaven, sometimes the Lady of the Sky. She is named the Lady of Heaven because she is recognized as a disembodied spirit being, or from the heavens, meaning she isn't from the earth. However, don't be deceived. She isn't from Heaven — the throne of God. She has been cast down to the lower chambers.

Ishtar is associated with sexual rites. Her cult would include worship in her temple with prostitution: the worshiper, primarily males but also females, engaged with the prostitute priests and priestesses in her temple.

The sexual engagement was meant to be a spiritual transfiguration by communing with spirits, not just the physical body of the gala priests or priestesses, but with the spirit-being Ishtar. Therefore, the temple prostitute was a conduit to the spirit world through sexual activity.

The ancient Mesopotamian goddess of love, war, and fertility is named Inanna, also known as Ishtar.

The Akkadians, Babylonians, and Assyrians primarily used the name Ishtar. The Greeks referred to her as Aphrodite, associated with Venus. Her characteristics as a goddess can be disgusting and grotesque.

When a man realizes whom he is competing with, he will not want to be in her sport. It's frightening and demeaning, and as stated earlier, it reduces a man to a piece of bread.

Let me describe the goddess, Ishtar. Once I do, you will recognize her in our culture and easily spot those channeling her spirit.

She is the Emasculator

She appears as an attractive and seductive woman yet has masculine attributes. Although beautiful, she is also a strong, brazen woman. She is bold and without shame. When needed, she will assume the role of the innocent to attract the male's ego, only to turn aggressive and domineering. She conflates both love and war into one. Her love is in the sense of lust, not the Biblical definition of love.

She can't be loved, so she seeks power.

She is a warrior woman. She is a fighter. She takes control by causing chaos. Rather than being submitted to male leadership, she leads; she dominates. Her jealousy is not *for* a man. She is jealous *of* men.

Ishtar is Unbridled

She does not want to be a bride, bound by the covenant of marriage. No, this spirit knows no bounds.

In mythology, Ishtar has a twin brother, Utu, with whom she has sexual relations. Incest is not out of bounds for Ishtar; it is paraded and celebrated. Utu is considered the god of divination and is associated with the underworld, the realm of the dead. His art is necromancy, communicating with the dead.

Ishtar is also non-binary. The priests in her temples, known as the *gala priests*, were non-binary, meaning gender-neutral. Males dressed as females and took female names, yet serviced male worshipers in her cult temples or sex centers. These gala priests were especially prone to dance in the temples. They were known for their carnival parades — colorful, prideful, and dressed in womanly costumes.

Likewise, today, our culture is being inundated with males

dressed as drag queens dancing at "family friendly" events that are even sponsored by the White House administration! They have their sights set on children, moving from transgenderism to pedophilia.

An ancient hymn of Ishtar declared, *"...make young women dress as men on their right side, to make young men dress on their left side."*

She wants to feminize men and make females masculine. Her goal is to alter the sexes. Confuse them. Rob them of their identity.

Are you getting the picture?

The spirit of Ishtar is emboldened in our culture — she is in our entertainment and has infiltrated our public education. She is influencing gender-neutral fashion. She is dominating our politics. She is combating cultural norms or, in the current term, "woke." You see her influence in the androgynous radicals rioting and causing chaos in the streets of our cities. She has millions of social media platforms. She is an influencer of keyboard warriors who attack and cancel anyone who dares to speak against her agenda.

She teaches her doctrine in songs. One pop star recently released a brazen song, *"I am not a woman, I'm a god/ I am not a martyr, I'm a problem/ I am not a legend, I'm a fraud."* The visuals in the music video are undeniable; she channels Ishtar in a temple.

In another song, she declares, *"If I can't have love, I want power."*

This is the bold and shameless ambition of Ishtar.

Ishtar can't find love, she wants power. She wants the power of men. One by one, she devours them like bread.

> ***An adulterous woman consumes a man, then wipes her mouth and says, "What's wrong with that?" —Proverbs 30:20 (New International Version)***
>
> ***Here's how a prostitute operates: she has sex with her client, Takes a bath, then asks, "Who's next?" — Proverbs 30:20 (Message)***

Another young artist (who grew up attending a church that I've preached in multiple times) sings, "*You, you love it how I move you/ You love it how I touch you / My one, when all is said and done/ You'll believe god is a woman.*"

I would not normally even mention those who are so blatantly blasphemous; however, it's important you see that Ishtar is a very real ***spirit being*** that is influencing Influencers.

Ishtar's lyrics indoctrinate children for the sake of her pedophilic dreams. Transgenderism isn't just about gender identity; the goal is to emasculate boys and mutilate girls.

Brothels and Ale Houses

Ishtar's cult centers became associated with brothels and beer houses.

In mythological tales, Ishtar seduces men with alcohol to get their "power" or what is referred to as "*meh* - a power which determines the laws of the universe and facilitates creation itself." One fantastical tale is when she wants to rob a man of his power, she goes to him, gets him intoxicated, and withdraws his power.

This seductive entrapment points to her desire to rob men of the original blessing, which is to be fruitful and multiply on the earth. She seems to hate God's first words over man. She despises that man is the source of the seed of life. She will take his seed only to flush it or abort it.

Play games with her. She will suck the life right out of you.

Ishtar attracts men to her Beer Houses and seduces them to her chambers, only to withdraw the power of their manhood. Proverbs gives us a description. As we look through the curtains of a window, we see how Ishtar seduces a young man.

> ***I saw some naive young men,***
> ***and one in particular who lacked common sense.***
> ***He was crossing the street near the house of an immoral woman,***
> ***strolling down the path by her house.***
> ***It was at twilight, in the evening,***

as deep darkness fell.
The woman approached him,
seductively dressed and sly of heart.
She was the brash, rebellious type,
never content to stay at home.
She is often in the streets and markets,
soliciting at every corner.
She threw her arms around him and kissed him,
and with a brazen look she said,
"I've just made my peace offerings
and fulfilled my vows.
You're the one I was looking for!
I came out to find you, and here you are!
My bed is spread with beautiful blankets,
with colored sheets of Egyptian linen.
I've perfumed my bed
with myrrh, aloes, and cinnamon.
Come, let's drink our fill of love until morning. — Proverbs 7:7-18 (New Living Translation)

How many men—countless, I suppose—have become impotent, losing their influence of authentic manhood, from the intoxication of alcohol and a loose dalliance with the whore?

Someone reading this will discard the book, tossing it in the trash because I've warned you about excessive drinking and exposing your vulnerability to be entrapped. There could be no better Proverb than this...

Faithful* are *the wounds of a friend,
But the kisses of an enemy* are *deceitful.* —*Proverbs

> ***27:6 (New International Version)***

This rebuke is coming from a friend. Her kisses are poisoned with deceit.

Porn is Sex with a Demon

> ***Surely her house leads down to death and her paths to the spirits of the dead. - Proverbs 2:18 (New International Version)***

We should personify the word *porn* because it means prostitute, and Ishtar is the spirit behind prostitution. She *is* the Prostitute.

Most men think that porn is the lesser of two evils. They think that adultery is a severe sin but porn is a manageable vice.

Porn is sex with a demon.

A disembodied spirit must inhabit a physical body to sexually commune with a man, which is adultery. However, if she can convince him to commune with her in his imagination he practices idolatry.

Porn takes adultery to the next level of sexual sin and becomes idolatry – communing with spirits.

Porn entices men to mingle with the demonic spirit, Ishtar.

I am being very direct and clear in this statement, but you must understand, the next time you look at porn you are having a sexual relationship with Ishtar, a demonic spirit of the underworld.

The next time you're tempted to gaze upon the images of Porn go ahead and say out loud, "I want to commune with Ishtar. I want to have sex with demons." That is exactly what you're doing. Every man she has slept with, every disease that ravages her, every filth of her being is now mingled with you.

Because that is what you're doing! You are bedding Ishtar!

You are having sex with a Demon.

Women who channel Ishtar

A casual examination of Hollywood starlets, singers, and models shows clearly who women are channeling to attract attention. I believe they often personify the goddess Ishtar. So desperate for attention, they sell their sex for men to lust after them.

I suspect they either knowingly, or at times out of ignorance or by counsel of others, dive into the characteristics of Ishtar. Likewise, some teach the arts of seduction and entrapment.

Balaam knew precisely how to entrap the Israelites. He created a doctrine on it. Many are teaching this doctrine of demons to young women today!

The definition of prostitution is using sex for financial gain. I will not demonize a woman and name the names of women this spirit uses. I don't suggest that you do either. Of course, different women come to mind, as many of them have channeled Ishtar's characteristics. They've used Ishtar to advance their career or for financial gain. They prostitute their physical attraction for personal gain.

My argument is not to arouse antipathy toward women.

Young men, I want to address those of you whom are identifying yourself as an *incel* (involuntary sexual abstinence). Incels are an online community of young men whose sexual advances are rejected by women. Hating women should not be the goal.

You should refrain from sex for the purpose of purity, with the expectation that you are qualifying yourself for a godly and pure wife.

You need to understand that Ishtar doesn't want to have sex with you but will if it reduces your status as an authentic man. She hates you.

An authentic man treats women gallantly, which will attract a lady.

I do not hate women. I love women. I respect women. I admire women. Women are the most beautiful and attractive of all of God's creations. God's greatest gift to man was the complementary design of a woman.

However, I despise the goddess of Ishtar. She manipulates women's innocence, purity, and attractiveness to do her bidding. Ishtar is obnoxious, loud, arrogant, classless, and most evil of all demonic spirits. She appears to be affectionate only to gain control and weaken men.

> ***It is shameful even to talk about the things that ungodly people do in secret. - Ephesians 5:12 (New International Version)***

I don't want to listen to what is done while bedding Ishtar. I honestly try to refrain from getting the details. I've heard enough. It's disheartening.

Yet occasionally, I do hear alarming, even frightening stories. As a speaker to tens of thousands of men each year, you can imagine the stories I've heard.

One man told me he visited a brothel disguised as a massage parlor, and while she was servicing him, he looked at her mouth. He told me, "Neil, it was as dark as tar; it seemed as if flies were coming out of her mouth. She would lick it up as the dark fluid dripped on her lips."

> ***The mouth of an adulterous woman is a deep pit; a man who is under the LORD's wrath falls into it. —Proverbs***

22:14 (New International Version)

He told me how scared he was, and realizing she was demonic, he hurriedly fled.

He repented.

I asked him what prompted him to go there in the first place.

His excuses were shallow. He told me how he had been disappointed in his marriage and disheartened toward God because of it. He stopped pursuing a relationship with God, no longer reading the Bible, skipping church services, and creating distance in what he knew was right.

I recall when Dr. Richard Dobbins, founder of Emerge Counseling Ministries, spoke at the seminary I attended. He had counseled hundreds of ministers who faced charges of moral failure. His conclusion was, "I've never counseled a minister who sinned sexually and had not previously stopped having prayer and devotional time with the Lord."

I noted what he said and determined that I would establish a discipline of reading the Word of God and having prayer time each morning.

However, listen carefully; no man can discipline himself to holiness. It is an issue of the heart.

"If my heart has been enticed by a woman, or if I have lurked at my neighbor's door, then may my wife grind

another man's grain, and may other men sleep with her. For that would have been wicked, a sin to be judged." - Job 31:9-11 (New International Version)

You can defeat the Prostitute. You can defeat Porn!

When David committed sexual sin, he cried, ***"Create in me a clean heart, O God; and renew a right spirit within me."*** (Psalm 51:10)

Confession of Faith

"I will not bed Ishtar!

I will not commune with evil spirits.

I refuse to be defeated by her.

I am not attracted to the Prostitute.

I will not be seduced by evil.

Her mouth is a deep, dark pit.

I will not descend into her.

My manhood is pure, strong, and powerful.

I make a covenant with my eyes, I will not be enticed by her.

The passions of my loins are reserved for the worthy woman, my wife.

I am strong. I am courageous. I am a man of God!"

3

The Heart of Man

> ***Whoever commits adultery with a woman lacks heart and understanding (moral principle and prudence); he who does it is destroying his own life. —Proverbs 6:32 (Amplified Classic Version)***

When a man responds to the lure of Ishtar, he *lacks heart*. Meaning that he lacks courage. He cowardly walks into her snare.

Porn is a Heart Matter

Most men have preconceived notions of the word *heart*. We need to define the word *heart* to understand the phrasing, *lacks heart*. Since we draw our understanding from the Word of God, the Bible, let us define heart from the Hebrew language to discover the original intent.

The Hebrew word heart is *leb*. The heart is the residence of the soul — mind, will, and emotions. It is the center of being. The moral character of his being is within the residence of man, for man is considered a Temple.

> **The heart is the seat of purposes, seat of appetites; seat of passions; seat of courage.**

When properly aligned, a man lives on purpose, which gives him meaning. Purpose provides a man with directional intent and dictates his appetite. **The WHY of his life governs WHAT he is craving.** He knows that God created him on purpose and for a purpose.

Your purpose determines your diet.

Growing up, my sport of choice was wrestling. If you know anything about wrestling, you know that cutting weight is a massive part of the sport. You must weigh in before each match. You will face an opponent of equal weight class. If you want to compete in wrestling, you will determine your diet.

In the same way, if you want to fulfill your purpose in life, you will dictate your diet. Your choices will be few. You will get on a nutritional program and manage it carefully.

When you know your WHY you will overcome WHAT you're craving.

Your appetites are designed to move you toward something. It causes your movement toward the goals of your purpose.

> ***The appetite of laborers works for them; their hunger drives them on. —Proverbs 16:26 (New International Version)***

Your appetite is good as long as you are craving righteousness and reaching to fulfill your destiny. As Jesus said, ***"Blessed are those who hunger and thirst for righteousness, for they shall be satisfied."*** (Matthew 5:6, English Standard Version)

The Apostle Paul said, ***"I press on to reach the end of the race and receive the heavenly prize for which God, through Christ Jesus, is calling us."*** (Philippians 3:14, New International Version)

When you understand your purpose you become passionate in pursuit of them. Your appetites add fuel to the fire. Then your passions give you the courage to face the challenges of your day.

Unfortunately, men often live passive, cowardly lives dominated by their flesh. Rather than the pursuit of purpose, their passions are often outbursts of anger, manic depression, fears, and irrational insecurities, often motivated by jealousy, causing fights and quarrels. Many have uncontrolled appetites, addictions, and bondage. They look for any sedation to relieve the stresses of life, up one minute, down the next — they're double-minded and unstable in all that they do. Their wives are insecure because they can't predict the behavior of their husbands, and their children lose confidence because of their father's inconsistency.

> ***Guard your heart above all else, for it determines the course of your life. —Proverbs 4:23 (New Living Translation)***

When a man is passive, emotionally unstable, and has uncontrolled appetites, he perverts his purpose.

As my friend, Dr. Myles Munroe, said, **"When the purpose is unknown, abuse is inevitable."**

In the following few chapters, I want to inspire and empower you to defeat the seductive trappings of this malevolent enemy spirit named Ishtar.

First, we must get our hearts calibrated. In other words, get your heart right and keep it right.

Are you a believer in and a follower of Christ?

I am not asking about accepting a religion, joining a branch of the Church, or buying into a fixer-upper-style spiritual makeover. I am asking if you've accepted Christ as your Lord, and are a disciple of His.

To be authentic, you must be a new man, first by repentance and then by discipleship. Don't let the word discipleship throw you off; it simply means that you are a follower of Jesus. He said, ***"I am the Way, the Truth, and the Life." (John 14:6 New International Version)***

If you follow Christ, He will show you the way. He will direct your steps. The steps of a righteous man are ordered. He gives us directional intent toward our destiny.

He will also keep you from deception. You will know the Truth and enjoy the freedom that comes with it. Having a clear mind is the superpower of our day. This culture is filled with deception, and knowing the Truth is vital to living authentically as a man.

He will give you an abundant Life. In Him was Life, and His Life is the light of men. Teaching the Word gives light, so even the simple can understand. Jesus does not make it complicated.

> ***Therefore, if anyone is in Christ, he is a new creation. The old has passed away; behold, the new has come. — 2 Corinthians 5:17 (New Living Translation)***

You can't fix up your old self. You can't discipline yourself to holiness. The Law served its purpose by pointing out the shortcomings of men; however, it never made anyone clean and righteous before God. This is not a make-over Gospel. It is a new beginning message.

Since you can't fulfill the Law, and since you can't clean up your mess, you must become a new creation.

> ***If you declare with your mouth, "Jesus is Lord," and believe in your heart that God raised him from the dead, you will be saved. - Romans 10:9 (New International Version)***

Notice where you must believe what you declare with your mouth. It is in your *heart*. So, you have a change of heart to become a new creation. It's called repentance.

Repent means to change one's mind for the better, *heartily* to amend with the abhorrence of one's past sins. When you believe in your heart that Jesus is Lord and make a verbal—speaking out loud—declaration of your belief, the Bible says that you are saved. When you are saved, you are made whole — delivered from the penalties of Law, recused from the Messianic judgments, resurrected from Death, and protected from the destructive efforts of the Evil ones.

It also means that you are no longer obligated to sin!

> ***Therefore, dear brothers and sisters, you have no obligation to do what your sinful nature urges you to do. - Romans 8:12 (New International Version)***

As a new man, you have your heart right; you're correctly aligned to fulfill your purpose and reach your destiny. The first step to defeat Ishtar is to repent in your heart and become a new man.

Prayer for Salvation

> ***"Father, I come to you in the Name of Jesus Christ, your Son, the Word who became flesh, the One crucified, the One who is the Resurrection and the Life. Have mercy on me. Create in me a clean heart. Sanctify me through your Word. It is with my heart that I believe. It is with my mouth that I declare, Jesus is Lord.***
>
> ***I am now born again. I am a new creation. Born of the Incorruptible Seed of God's Word. I will never be the same. Old things have passed away. There is now, no condemnation against me. There is no unsettled claim in my life. I have believed in Him. I have received***

Him. Therefore, I am a son of God, who has the power to become.

As a new man, cleansed from all iniquity, I walk in righteousness. I make godly decisions because I have the mind of Christ. My mind is renewed. His thoughts are higher than my thoughts. His ways are superior to my ways. I lean on Him, not on myself for support. I cast down vain imaginations. I no longer play with fantasies.

He has given me the Holy Spirit to live within me, baptizing me with cleansing fire, and purifying my innermost being. I am filled with the Spirit. I am a Temple of the Holy, authorized Spirit. I will not join my body, the residence of the Holy Spirit with a prostitute.

Now, I choose to live on purpose and for His purposes that He created for me. My appetites hunger and thirst for righteousness. My passions are the fuel that moves me toward a higher calling in Christ Jesus. I am a strong and courageous man. I fear no man.

I choose purity and holiness, meaning I am set apart for God's purposes. I passionately pursue God's purposes for my life. I will reach my destiny, in Jesus' Name. Amen!"

Now, let's put Ishtar back in her place! She belongs in the underworld, and that is where we will send her. Get ready for a spiritual fight.

He shall not be afraid of evil tidings: his heart is fixed, trusting in the LORD. —Psalm 112:7 (King James Ver-

sion)

4

The Seat of Purpose

The purposes of a man's heart are deep waters, but a man of understanding draws them out. - Proverbs 20:5

If you've read my book, **FivestarMan**, you know that Proverbs 20:5 is our foundational precept. If you haven't, I want to send you a free copy. Go to **FivestarManBook.com**.

Solomon describes the purposes in our hearts as deep waters. Again, the residence of purposes is within your heart. In the book, **FivestarMan**, I give an understanding of five categories of God's original design and intent of a man, thus authentic manhood. FivestarMan is not the measurement of your manhood. Every man has all five purposes within him. You're not a one, two, three, four, or five-star man in ranking; you are a FivestarMan because they already reside within you.

Understanding Draws Out Your Purposes

I want to give you a quick overview, although I strongly recommend that you get the book, **FivestarMan,** to gain even more understanding of your purposes.

You were made ON purpose. You were made FOR a purpose.

Your purposes are not hidden on the heights of mountains forcing you to scale. The peak of Everest does not offer a golden box for you to open and discover the secrets of your purposes.

> ***No one can know a person's thoughts except that person's spirit, and no one can know God's thoughts except God's own Spirit. —1 Corinthians 2:11***

Paul tells us that God has secret wisdom that this world doesn't comprehend. He points out that you do not discover these secrets by what you see, by what you hear, nor by the schemes of your imagination. He says this wisdom from above is already within your spirit.

God is not keeping secrets FROM you. God is keeping secrets FOR you.

I hope you're meditating on the profound truth that the secrets of your purposes are not challenging to discover. However, you will need understanding to draw them out.

The Purposes of a Man

The first word for ***man*** is Adam which means ***mankind***. He doesn't use the proper name, Adam, until Genesis 2:19, when he is given the authority to name the animals. After naming them and positioning dominion over them, God says, *"It is not good for Adam to be alone."*

God performs a surgical extraction of the bone to use for forming Adam's help meet. The Woman is formed into the perfect complementary design.

(Please do not jump to the theological argument of complementarian versus egalitarianism. That is not my argument here, nor is it applicable. I am using that term to describe the perfection of God's design for a woman to complement the design of a man and vice versa.)

Once again, Adam called her by her name, and her name is purposed, *Woman*.

Woman is *'ishshâh*, the feminine version of the man.

Remember that God extracted the bone and formed the Woman from the man. She came from him. He no longer had mankind within him. He is now the male, and she is the female. In other words, I suggest that the feminine portion of mankind is no longer within the male. For a man to benefit from the help meet, he must have the complement of a wife.

The purposes of a man's heart are deep waters, but a

man of understanding draws them out. - Proverbs 20:5 (New International Version 1984 Edition)

In this Proverb, the word for man is *Iysh. Iysh* is a masculine male as opposed to a woman. Within the word Iysh, you discover incredible descriptive words, such as champion, husband, cultivator, mighty, citizen, a man of God, priest, companion, warrior, gallant, valiant, chivalry, intelligent, celebrated, nobleman, and legend.

I took these terms and categorized them into the compounded word of FivestarMan.

I want to be very clear, my goal in speaking to men about these five purposes is not to conform them to what I believe a man of God should be. I am speaking directly to the purposes that are already within them.

We do a disservice to God and men by attempting to fashion them (literally) after our imagination of manhood. I've certainly been in enough conference rooms and committees with men who thought they knew best what a man should be and how he should dress and behave. However, man-made edicts do not work.

> **Who you are and what you are called to be is best defined by your Creator.**

Yet you, LORD, are our Father. We are the clay, you are the potter; we are all the work of your hand. —Isaiah 64:8 (New International Version)

One pastor noted while I was speaking about being an authentic man, FivestarMan that men stopped slouching in their seats, changing their posture, and began to lean into the message. He said, "Neil, I saw you draw out the purposes that are within the men!"

The emotions of men erupt from their purposes! I've seen it thousands of times. Each time I speak to men about the message of authentic manhood, I know the watering of their eyes. Their emotions begin to boil up as if they are going to burst like hot springs.

Adventurous Spirit

> ***Benaiah son of Jehoiada, a valiant fighter from Kabzeel, performed great exploits. He struck down Moab's two mightiest warriors. He also went down into a pit on a snowy day and killed a lion. — 2 Samuel 23:20 (New International Version)***

Within every man is an adventurous spirit. You must have it. The adventurous spirit gives you the ability to take risks for the rewards of life. As David said, *"What will be done for the man?"* (1 Samuel 17:26)

Men relate with other men differently than women relate with other women.

Men relate shoulder-to-shoulder facing a challenge.

Our relationships are forged on the fields of the contest. Football fields. Soccer fields. Baseball fields. Or even battlefields. Men develop relationships on the field.

I noticed this when I pastored my first church. It seemed as if every man whom I counseled face-to-face in my office eventually left my church. I thought I must be a horrible counselor and even looked into pursuing my degree in counseling to make up for my lack of skill. I was ignorant of relating to men.

However, I also noticed when I related to men on a field of contest, such as golf, we created lifelong friendships and brotherhood.

> You must draw upon your adventurous spirit and stay engaged on the field of the contest.

David was a man of adventure. He fought a lion to protect his father's sheep. He rescued the sheep from an attacking bear. When God needed a shepherd for His people, he saw what David did in secret and promoted him publicly.

David fought Goliath on the public stage. He wasn't cowardly. The movies never portray him correctly. David said to Goliath, ***"This day, the Lord will deliver you into my hands, and I'll strike you down and cut off your head. This day I will give the carcasses of the Philistine army to the birds and the wild animals, and the whole world will know that there is a God in Israel."*** (1 Samuel 17:46)

David wasn't just going after Goliath; he was calling out the entire Philistine army.

David won every battle that he ever fought. Except one.

The Balcony of Boredom

When David became a seasoned king, his counselors feared for his life. They considered that he was too precious to fight on the field of the contest. He listened to their horrible counsel.

In the spring, at the time when kings go off to war, David stayed at home. This proved to be a costly mistake. Kings are meant to lead their men on the field of the contest, not sit at home in the comforts of the couch.

You can imagine the discourse in David's mind. He had been a warrior. The girls of Israel wrote and sang songs about him. He was the most admired man in the nation.

Wandering on the balcony, David is bored and then sees her. A bathing woman.

What would she feel like? What would she smell like? What would she taste like? Questions raced through his imagination. He wanted the affection that comes with the caress. He wanted the conquering of her. He felt entitled to her.

You know the story.

All because David withdrew from the field of the contest. All because he wandered on the balcony. All because he was bored.

Bored Men Sin

You are not designed to settle. You are made for action. Don't be seduced by the sofa.

Get up and get moving.
Recondition your body.
Reengage your activity.
Reinvest your energy.

Entrepreneurial Drive

> ***Then the Lord said to Moses, "Look, I have specifically chosen Bezalel son of Uri, grandson of Hur, of the tribe of Judah. I have filled him with the Spirit of God, giving him great wisdom, ability, and expertise in all kinds of crafts. He is a master craftsman, an expert in working with gold, silver, and bronze. He is skilled in engraving and mounting gemstones and in carving wood. He is a master at every craft! —Exodus 31:1–5 (New International Version)***

You have within you an entrepreneurial drive. This is a fantastic gift that God has established within you, guaranteeing your ability to be your own economy. I firmly believe that every man has a unique skill set that God has given him. I also think that his skill can be sharpened and commercialized.

> ***Now to each one the manifestation of the Spirit is given for the common good. —1 Corinthians 12:7 (New Living Translation)***

I am aware I am using this scripture out of its context. However, I hope you can see the universality of its truth. Your gift is for the common good.

God created you to be a cultivator. His first gift to mankind was the gift of seed. With seed, every man could determine his diet and satisfy his cravings. (I will speak more on this in the next chapter.) For now, understand that the seed laid dormant on the Earth until Adam was placed in the Garden to work it.

Yes, I said work. Work is not part of the curse; work is a blessing. God gave Adam a job before He gave him a wife or helped meet.

There is no need for a help meet if you don't have a job.

The job that God gave to Adam was to cultivate the Garden with the desired seeds that were provided. It was a vocation, meaning a Divine calling.

Your job isn't meant to be labor; it is intended to be a calling.

Gallant Relationships

> ***Treat older women as you would your mother, and treat younger women with all purity as you would your own sisters. 1 Timothy 5:2 (New International Version)***

A line between respect and familiarity governs every relationship. Respect honors the value and distinction of another person. Familiarity in the negative sense treats a person as ordinary or insignificant.

As authentic men, we should treat older women as our mothers. We should treat younger women as our daughters. We should treat our peers as sisters.

Every woman that is used in porn is someone's daughter or sister. If we governed our relationships, we would consider them valuable and worthy of honor.

The only woman who should receive the intimacies of our eyes and the passions of our loins is our wives.

Faithful in Character

> ***Guard my life, for I am faithful to you; save your servant who trusts in you. You are my God. —Psalm 86:2 (New International Version)***

In the original language, the phrase faithful reads, "*for I am a godly man.*" The Psalmist is singing to the Lord, "Guard me! Put a hedge of protection around me, for I am a godly man."

As godly men, we want to live faithfully to the Lord. We want to be men of integrity and authenticity. We're not fearful, weak little boys. We're men of God! We want to be faith-filled.

> ***Follow the steps of good men instead, and stay on the paths of the righteous. — Proverbs 2:20 (New Living Translation)***

Your steps are ordered to stay on the paths of righteousness.

Philanthropic in Cause

> ***Yet God has made everything beautiful for its own time. He has planted eternity in the human heart, but even so, people cannot see the whole scope of God's work from beginning to end. —Ecclesiastes 3:11***

I love this verse. God planted eternity in a man's heart. The King James Version says, ***"God set the world in their hearts."*** As an authentic man, you're not living just for today—your purpose-driven for eternity.

Most men are only thinking about success. Authentic men think in terms of significance.

Your success can not be measured by someone else. Only you can define what success is for you. However, significance can only be measured by how your life impacts others. You cannot determine if you've been significant.

As you discover your entrepreneurial hand to gather resources, your philanthropic hand scatters to others.

Success is measured by gain. Significance is determined by giving.

This is what tripped up the rich young ruler who approached Jesus. He was rich and very successful at a young age. He was a leader among his peers. Yet, he lacked something. Jesus picked up on it immediately and gave the young man an opportunity to become significant.

Unfortunately, the young man failed the test. His success made him comfortable.

The greatest temptation is comfort.

Becoming comfortable in the level of success you have achieved and not reaching higher can also threaten your significance. You can always achieve more and give more.

As authentic men, we want to live and leave a legacy. My goal is to hear my children tell their children, "We serve the God of my father." If I hear that, the legacy of faith will be more valuable than any amount of financial inheritance I will leave them.

> ***A good man leaves an inheritance to his children's children, but the sinner's wealth is laid up for the righteous. —Proverbs 13:22 (English Standard Version)***

These five purposes give you directional intent. If you live to fulfill them, you will not have time for trivial pursuits.

5

The Seat of Appetites

But Jeshurun soon became fat and unruly; the people grew heavy, plump, and stuffed! Then they abandoned the God who had made them; they made light of the Rock of their salvation. They stirred up his jealousy by worshiping foreign gods; they provoked his fury with detestable deeds. They offered sacrifices to demons, which are not God, to gods they had not known before, to new gods only recently arrived, to gods their ancestors had never feared. —Deuteronomy 32:15 (New Living Translation)

Jeshurun means upright one. It is used as a term of endearment, a loving term that refers to Israel's ideal character. Yet, what follows is the description of Israel's uncontrolled appetites.

Before he departs from leadership, Moses prophesies to his beloved Israel. Listen to what he says. Israel's ideal character became fat, unruly, heavy, plump, and stuffed! *Then* they abandoned the God who made them and worshiped foreign gods.

Unconditioned Men

If you haven't stopped reading this book, you may after what I am about to say. However, if you will read it, this book could save your life and eternal destiny.

You cannot afford to grow fat.

Earlier I said what you do physically affects you spiritually. And, what you do spiritually affects you physically.

Food Became a Comforter

When I faced challenges and became stressed by what I was attempting to accomplish, I often turned to food as a comfort rather than relying on the Comforter of the Holy Spirit. I am not saying that to sound spiritual. On the contrary, it shows precisely where my lid of spirituality was.

Turning to comfort food made me hit the scales over 250 pounds.

My wife became very concerned. She hid it well. She has always been kind to me and supportive. However, she wondered what she would do without me. She knew I was on a fast track to poor health that might cost me my life. She felt the Holy Spirit prompt her to speak to me about getting on a plan. She said to the Spirit, "OK, I will mention it, but if Neil rejects it, I am not asking again."

When she mentioned it, I abruptly said, "No."

That night, I awakened at 3am to pray, which is not unusual for me. I was expecting my routine of intercessory prayer when I strongly felt the Holy Spirit's conviction saying, "Neil, you've had two friends die prematurely because they did not have the physical conditioning to finish their purpose in life. Not everyone can say they've finished their race. Some can't say that because they did not condition themselves for their race. You will have a third friend die next week."

I knew this was a warning for me. I knew two men, great men, who were doing incredible works for the Lord, who died before their time. The following week, a third died suddenly of a heart condition due to his morbid obesity.

The following day, I stopped Kay before she went out the door for her morning walk. I committed to reconditioning my body and reclaiming my health. I found a plan that I've seen work in others' lives. I got on the plan and worked it. I didn't play games with it. My daily confession was Psalm 119:29, "**Keep me from lying to myself**; give me the privilege of knowing your instructions."

In six months, I lost 70-pounds, and I've kept it off for two years.

(If you need to get on a plan, reach out to me at Neil@Fivestar-Man.com. I will share with you what worked for me.)

Within the first few days of the plan, my brain fog had lifted. My emotions were stabilized. My energy for life returned. Soon, the fat began to disappear. Who knew that determining my diet would affect my spiritual life so much?

I should have known that food affects us spiritually because the Bible repeatedly gives us direction for repentance, beginning with fasting.

What you do physically affects you spiritually. What you do spiritually affects you physically.

I did not realize how dull my spirit had become and how food sedated me from the voice of the Holy Spirit.

> ***You say, "Food for the stomach and the stomach for food, and God will destroy them both." The body, however, is not meant for sexual immorality but for the Lord, and the Lord for the body. — 1 Corinthians 6:13 (New International Version)***

Paul points out that our appetites play a role in our sexual immorality. Again, the word immorality is *porneia* — which refers to the worship of idols.

Remember, the sin at Acacia Grove involved eating foods sacrificed to idols.

> ***He taught them to sin by eating food offered to idols and by committing sexual sin. - Revelation 2:14 (New International Version)***

When we desire food more than we desire our destiny, we become bloated and fat.

> ***Their destiny is destruction, their god is their stomach, and their glory is in their shame. Their mind is set on earthly things. —Philippians 3:19 (New International Version)***

To defeat Ishtar (Porn), you must commit to reconditioning your body and calibrating your heart.

This is a subject that very few in the Church have been willing to tackle, but I am not here to appease you, comfort you in your sedation, or pat you on the head and say, "You're a good boy." I hope to provoke you to excellence so you will live up to your potential and reach your destiny.

> ***Let us think of ways to motivate one another to acts of love and good works. —Hebrews 10:24 (New Living Translation)***

I am writing this because I've seen the destruction. I've seen friends die too early. I've also noticed that uncontrolled appetites pervert purposes.

> ***Flee from sexual immorality. All other sins a person commits are outside the body, but whoever sins sexually, sins against their own body. —1 Corinthians 6:18 (New International Version)***

Again, notice the synergy between sexual immorality (Porn) and the body. The interaction is undeniable. Food affects your sexual appetite as well as your physical body.

I've known men who wanted to be wanted. They craved the affection of a woman's desire for them. Yet, their physical appearance is such that women are no longer attracted to them—and this applies particularly to a man's wife losing her attraction to him. To satisfy their desire these men either fantasize about Ishtar (Porn) or purchase a woman for her seductive, faked affection.

Paying for affection to reach five minutes of satisfaction. What a sad commentary on a man's life.

Their god is their appetite. Their glory is in their shame.

> ***It's the same when you have sex with your neighbor's wife: Touch her and you'll pay for it. No excuses. Hunger is no excuse for a thief to steal; When he's caught he has to pay it back, even if he has to put his whole house in hock. Adultery is a brainless act, soul-destroying, self-destructive; Expect a bloody nose, a black eye, and a reputation ruined for good. — Proverbs 6:30-32 (Message Version)***

Proverbs says, "*Hunger is no excuse.*"

Solomon also recognizes how an appetite motivates a man. Then he says it's a brainless act, soul-destroying, and self-destructive.

> ***See that no one is sexually immoral, or is godless like Esau, who for a single meal sold his inheritance rights as the oldest son. —Hebrews 12:6 (New International***

> ***Version)***

Once again, you see the connection between the sexually immoral and uncontrolled appetite of Esau. Esau exchanged his destiny for a single meal.

> ***Afterward, as you know, when he wanted to inherit this blessing, he was rejected. Even though he sought the blessing with tears, he could not change what he had done. —Hebrews 12:7 (New International Version)***

Tears alone do not represent repentance. Esau and Judas are both known for their tears but did not have spiritual repentance.

Ishtar's Intoxication

Ishtar seduces men with alcohol to get their "power" or what is referred to as "*meh* - a power which determines the laws of the universe and facilitates creation itself." In the ancient poem about her seduction of Enki, she uses alcohol to seduce him so she can steal from him his power. He held these secret powers of masculinity. She wanted them.

As we are encouraged not to be ignorant of Satan's devices or schemes, we must also be aware of Ishtar's tricks and entrapment. She uses our appetite for merriment to sedate us, making us vulnerable to seduction.

> ***Be sober-minded, be alert. Your adversary the devil is prowling around like a roaring lion, looking for anyone he can devour. —1 Peter 5:8***

Earlier, in chapter 4:7, Peter explains that we should be sober-minded and alert because the end of all things is near. He connects our present with the nearness of our destiny. Then he reminds us to be sober-minded because the adversary prowls like a lion.

In the temples of Ishtar, lions were used as symbols for her hunting nature. She is known to be always on the hunt. She is never satisfied. She wants to conquer.

The words adversary and devil describe the slander that comes with sexual sin. As an adversary might bring a legal case against someone, Ishtar is looking for a man she can tarnish with a defamatory suit. She will chew on him like bread, then vomit his reputation.

Young men, keep your cool. Stay alert. Don't get caught off guard. How many young men have been destroyed early in their lives because of one night of drunkenness?

It's not just for young men. Seasoned men take warning. Lot and Noah were both disadvantaged because they gave themselves over to intoxication. Noah had one night of drunkenness that exposed his son, Ham, to a generational curse. Lot's daughters got him drunk and had sexual relations with him which resulted in generations of evil.

Again, I know that some of you may be angry with me because I have confronted an addiction, but wounds from a friend can be trusted. Please understand my motivation. I am not saying that wine and beer are forbidden in Scripture. They are not banned.

However, it is also clear that drinking excessively can and will be destructive to you. They are gates of opportunity for destructive behaviors.

The Witchcraft of Drugs

> ***When you follow the desires of your sinful nature, the results are very clear: sexual immorality, impurity, lustful pleasures, idolatry, sorcery, hostility, quarreling, jealousy, outbursts of anger, selfish ambition, dissension, division, envy, drunkenness, wild parties, and other sins like these. —Galatians 5:19 (New International Version)***

The word for sorcery is the word for drugs.

Few men realize that *Pharmakeia* can refer to drugs, potions, spells, poisonings, witchcraft, and magical potions.

Let me first share a disclaimer. I am NOT speaking against the practice of healing arts or medical sciences, nor am I against using medicines that help recover a sick person. The Bible speaks well of physicians (Matthew 9:12; Mark 2:7; Luke 5:31).

My concern is when drugs are used for recreational purposes that cause intoxication, fuel sedation, or cause someone to lose control of their mental, emotional, or spiritual senses.

We've already established that sexual immorality is the word Porn. We've also shared that when a man copulates with Ishtar (Porn), he practices idolatry — sexually communing with an evil spirit.

The next word listed in Galatians 5:19 is sorcery, or *Pharmakeia*, meaning the use of drugs, deceptions, and seductions of idolatry.

Drugs are a gateway to idolatry.

Ishtar uses a witches' brew to seduce. She uses drugs to sedate. To steal power from men.

Do not be arbitrary when it comes to digesting chemicals in your body. You must be doing so on purpose and for a purpose. You must be alert and sober-minded in these last days.

My best friend from high school is on death row for murder. He became addicted to crystal-methamphetamine. What started as a way for him to work long hours soon became the reason he was fired from a very high-paying job. He then began to sell meth to make money. I don't know the facts of his case. All I know is he was tried and convicted for murdering a friend.

I looked deep into his eyes when I visited and prayed with him. I could barely recognize my friend. The drugs altered his physical appearance and scarred his soul. I remember him as the young, good-looking, fun guy in high school. Now, he was a defeated addict and murderer.

Don't Become Stuffed with Pride

> ***When you have eaten and are satisfied, praise the Lord your God for the good land he has given you. —Deuteronomy 8:10 (New International Version)***

Israel was warned about the temptation of comfort. They were to be very careful not to become complacent.

- Be careful that you do not forget the Lord.
- Don't fail to observe the precepts, principles of the law, and God's decrees.
- Make sure that you put into practice the Words of God.

The greatest temptation in a man's life is comfort.

I've seen it a thousand times. Men reach a certain level of comfort and become arrogant and ungrateful. They become entitled.

> ***Otherwise, when you eat and are satisfied, when you build fine houses and settle down, and when your herds and flocks grow large and your silver and gold increase and all you have is multiplied, then your heart will become proud and you will forget the Lord your God, who brought you out of Egypt, out of the land of slavery.***
> ***—Deuteronomy 8:12–14 (New International Version)***

Do you see the warning about the appetite?
"When you eat and are satisfied....."
"...then your heart will become proud, and you will forget...."

You must be careful when you succeed!

Men, please, please, listen to me. I've seen many men who start with nothing; they achieve a measure of success and soon forget where they came from and who they are.

> ***If you ever forget the Lord your God and follow other gods and worship and bow down to them, I testify against you today that you will surely be destroyed. — Deuteronomy 8:19 (New International Version)***

As always, the warning is when your stomach is satisfied, you are often seduced by evil spirits — other gods. **Pride attracts Ishtar like a magnet attracts metal.**

Your heart is the seat of appetites. As we calibrate our heart, the seat of appetites, let's hunger and thirst for righteousness.

Pray this Prayer

"Father, I hunger and thirst for righteousness. I crave the goodness of God. I am grateful for what you've done in my life. I choose to seek you. As a man, I do not live on food alone, but I live on the Word of God. I commit my body to the conditioning of my purposes. I choose to deny myself. I am satisfied with you. My mind is alert. I am sober-minded. I choose my appetites. I know my destiny. In Jesus' Name, Amen."

6

The Seat of Passions

> ***I discovered that a seductive woman is a trap more bitter than death. Her passion is a snare, and her soft hands are chains. Those who are pleasing to God will escape her, but sinners will be caught in her snare. — Ecclesiastes 7:26 (New Living Translation)***

A seductive woman's heart is a snare. Her hands are chains. Her passions are a trap. She doesn't love you. She never will. It is not in her nature to love. She is motivated by one thing — she wants to steal the power of your manhood and reduce you to bread.

Men are often deceived into imagining they have captured the heart of the Harlot, the spirit of Prostitution, who is Ishtar. However, her trap is bitterness.

Your passion for authentic manhood must be greater than her passion for conquering you. You can escape her snare and entanglement of her hands by pleasing the Lord.

You Can Escape

Within your heart are passions. A passionate man is powerful when he is pursuing his purposes. Your desires will be fueled by your appetites when correctly aligned with your destiny. The energy and motivation of your life will seem unstoppable.

When making decisions, most people determine their decision by their emotions. How will this make me feel?

If you choose your behavior based on emotions, you will be unstable in everything you do. Emotions should result from your purposes, not the determining factor that guides your life.

When you live on purpose, you dictate your appetites and are fueled by your passions. If you live by emotions, you will have uncontrolled appetites and pervert your purposes.

Emotion is a relatively new word, dating back to 1579, meaning *"to stir up."*

> ***Therefore I remind you <u>to stir up</u> the gift of God which is in you through the laying on of my hands. —2 Timothy 1:6 (New King James Version)***

Other versions say, *"fan into flames the gift of God."*

In other words, you can control the fire of your passions. If you can choose to stir up, you're in control. The gift of God, the

Spiritual deposit of your purposes, and empowerment are at your discretion.

Men, when the spirit of Ishtar is enticing you, you can escape her seduction by stirring up your gift. Align your passions with your purposes.

Spew the Bitter Morsels

> ***See to it that no one falls short of the grace of God and that no bitter root grows up to cause trouble and defile many. —Hebrews 12:15 (New International Version)***

I've known men who had arguments with their wives and swallowed bitterness that took root in their emotions. Things didn't go as planned, so rather than be mature men and deal with it, they, in effect, acted like emotional babies and pouted because they didn't get their way.

Don't swallow the bitter morsels.

Uncontrolled Anger

> **Anger is cruel and fury overwhelming, but who can stand before jealousy? — Proverbs 27:4**

Do not allow the day to pass without ridding yourself of anger. Anger digs deep into the soul of man. It can draw out buried emotions from years past in an instant. We must distinguish the different types of anger and extinguish the harmful emotions.

The Four Faces of Anger

- **RAGE** is a fit of anger that causes us to flurry about with over-expressed gestures, clenched jaws, boisterous words, and even calling down curses. This kind of anger typically comes from frustrated expectations. Expressing rage causes people around you to stare at you in disbelief, confusion, or embarrassment.
- **FURY** is a much stronger emotion of rage. It is a deadly form of madness, often leading to a depraved mind and delusional violence. Fury is motivated by evil. This often results in physical harm to others, even murder.
- **INDIGNATION** is righteous anger caused by witnessing or experiencing injustice, shame, or evil done to innocence. Indignation motivates men to protect and risk their lives for the cause of others. It is the correct use of the emotion of anger.
- **WRATH** is the godliest form of anger. It is anger that responds to evil with pure judgment. Wrath causes a man to correct a wrong and to rid the earth of evil.

Some men have been taught to sequester their anger and be stoic in emotions, yet anger has a role in our lives if our motivations are pure and our response is disciplined.

Jealousy is the extreme energy of anger expressed by an envious person. Solomon says that jealousy is the most destructive of all forms of anger. It is the motivation for innumerable murders, sexual crimes, and violence.

Insecurity

Insecure men are dangerous.

I believe insecurity is caused when a man doesn't know WHO he is in Christ.

Unfortunately, we have an epidemic of fatherless homes in our culture. The repercussions are alarming. I could overwhelm you with the statistics, but most of us have personal experiences in this area in one way or another.

A fatherless boy feels the vulnerability of a lack of protection. Not having a covering of authority exposes him to all kinds of evil. Often sexual molestation, verbal abuse, bullying, or economic insecurity all play a role in shaping his lack of confidence when he becomes a man.

Even when a man becomes a Christian, in many cases, he often transfers his father wound to see God, the Father, in the same perspective of abandonment.

I can't tell you how often men have traced their addiction to Porn to the vulnerability of not having a father. Get a copy of my book entitled, *Pray Like a Son*. It will help you understand who your Father is and how to have a relationship with Him.

I've often shared how my father left our home when I was five. I know the vulnerability of not having a father. I know the confusion of having my identity stolen from me as a child.

However, if you know me as a man, you may know that I walk with confidence in who I am in Christ. My assurance is not in my flesh. It is solely on the knowledge of my relationship with Christ and love for my *Abba*, Father.

Sexless Marriages

I rarely share any information I gather from counseling others. I certainly will not break confidentiality. However, a cultural phenomenon has happened in our lifetime. In an age of sexuality, many marriages are sexless. They have no passion for one another.

A couple sat down with me to discuss their marriage. The couple had all of the appearances of success. They made enormous amounts of money. They lived in a beautiful home. They took care of themselves physically and dressed with precision. They also confessed Christ as Savior.

Then the bombshell. In eight years of marriage, they had sexual intimacy twice.

I couldn't hold my astonishment. "What?!" I replied. "You mean this week?"

Since then, I have discovered this is more of the norm than the exception.

> ***Do not deprive each other of sexual relations, unless you both agree to refrain from sexual intimacy for a limited time so you can give yourselves more completely***

> ***to prayer. Afterward, you should come together again so that Satan won't be able to tempt you because of your lack of self-control. —1 Corinthians 7:5 (New Living Translation)***

You cannot have a thriving marriage without physical passions.

Your Passions Can Move You

God has placed passions within you. Drawing upon them properly can move you toward your destiny.

> ***Never be lacking in zeal, but keep your spiritual fervor, serving the Lord. —Romans 12:11 (New International Version)***

The word for zeal and spiritual fervor means diligence. We must be consistent and committed to our efforts to pursue our purposes.

My personal mission is to live proficiently in Biblical faith, love, health, and prosperity. I want to prove diligent in my efforts to please the Lord.

To fulfill my personal mission, I have established diligent routines.

- Read the through the Bible every 90-Days.
- Pray every morning, evening, and often at 3 am for intercessory prayer
- Keep a gratitude journal

- Keep a vision board
- Listen to sermons and teachings of various ministers and ministries
- Pray with my wife
- Attend Church services

Pray this Prayer

"Father, I want to please you. I want to escape the bitter trap of Ishtar. I choose to stir up the gift of God that is within me. My mind is alert to her deception. My heart is fixed on You. My spirit is stirred with passion for my purposes. My flesh is crucified with Christ. I will NOT join my manhood with the Harlot. In Jesus' Name, Amen!"

7

The Seat of Courage

Be of good courage, and let us play the men for our people, and for the cities of our God: and the LORD do that which seemeth him good. —2 Samuel 10:12 (King James Version)

I've devoted the last twelve years to encouraging men to step up to the high calling of authentic manhood. During this time, I've discovered that we're not facing the challenge of toxic masculinity. Mainly because what society is calling harmful, we're calling authentic. What we call toxic is what they seem to prefer.

Our society, specifically the Church, has suffered from passivity or cowardice in men.

David sent ambassadors to the heir apparent of the Ammonites, Hanun. Rejecting David's gesture of peace, Hanun accosted the ambassadors and humiliated them. David does not allow this insult to go without action. He sends his warriors to battle.

The Ammonites were descendants of incestual relations and worshiped the detestable god, Moloch, or as we saw earlier, in the name of their cousins' god, Chemosh. In fear, they hire 20,000 Arameans and another 13,000 from other sources.

Joab and his brother, Abishai, lead David's army to battle. Joab says to the men, *"Be of good courage, and let us play the men...."*

There are times in our lives when we either step up and be a man, or we shrink back into obscurity.

Joab is motivating his men to fight for the people of God and the cities of God! In other words, we need to find the mettle within us which defines us as men.

Listen, you must realize that we're in a real battle against an enemy that wants to destroy you.

Why is Ishtar, the spirit of prostitution, being used against you? Because you're a man! Because you are the protector of everything, dear...

Your wife.
Your children.
Your church.
Your community.
Your city.
Your country.

You're a coward if you do not aggressively protect those you love and what you have.

> ***For husbands, this means love your wives, just as Christ loved the church. He gave up his life for her to make her holy and clean, washed by the cleansing of God's word. —Ephesians 5:25 (New International Version)***

It is vital that men cast off the restraints and take a leading role in the affairs of our families, church, and communities. To do so, we must leave passivity and courageously fight a good fight of faith.

Passivity accepts what happens without an active response.

Bind the Strong Man, Rob the House

> ***Every kingdom divided against itself will be ruined, and every city or household divided against itself will not stand. If Satan drives out Satan, he is divided against himself. How then can his kingdom stand? And if I drive out demons by Beelzebul, by whom do your people drive them out? So then, they will be your judges. But if it is by the Spirit of God that I drive out demons, then the kingdom of God has come upon you.***
>
> ***Or again, how can anyone enter a strong man's house and carry off his possessions unless he first ties up the strong man? Then he can plunder his house. —Matthew 12:25-29 (New International Version)***

The Pharisees accuse Jesus of using Satan to drive out demons. It's a blasphemous accusation against the Spirit of God. Jesus teaches two very important lessons.

1. A house divided against itself cannot stand.
2. A house cannot be robbed unless the strong man, the protector of the home, is not first bound.

The first principle is widely accepted and has been used to rally the troops to unity. Pastors have used it extensively to encourage unity in the Church. Certainly, we have appropriated it to understand that a family will not stay together if they disagree.

The second principle is often misunderstood.

The word "strong man" is *ischyros,* which means strong, violent, firm, and sure. It also means one who has the strength of the soul to sustain the attacks of Satan, strong and therefore exhibiting excellence.

Satan comes only to steal, kill, and destroy (John 10:10). He wants to rob you of your possessions. You must be courageous enough to go to battle and show yourself to be a man.

You are the Strong Man

The evil ambition of Ishtar is to steal everything that you hold dear. She is not a lover; she is a foe. Ishtar wants you dead. Ishtar wants to destroy you.

Yes, her soft hands are claws that will squeeze the life out of your manhood. She will mock you and laugh at your shame.

Say this out loud...
"I will not bed Ishtar."

Repeat it...
"I will not bed Ishtar."

Now say it louder...
"I WILL NOT BED ISHTAR!"

When you know your purpose, you will dictate your appetites.

When you dictate your appetites, you will fuel your passions.

When you fuel your passions, you will have the courage to face your challengers.

Accountability Versus Agreement

> ***That does not mean we want to dominate you by telling you how to put your faith into practice. We want to work together with you so you will be full of joy, for it is by your own faith that you stand firm. —2 Corinthians 1:24***

In the above scripture, the Apostle Paul is revealing that each man will only **stand firm** by the practice of his own faith. He is acknowledging that God gave man dominion over the earth, **not domination** over other men.

> ***O LORD our God, other lords beside thee have had dominion over us: but by thee only will we make mention of thy name. — Isaiah 26:13 (King James***

Version)

When you serve the Lord, God, no one is to have dominion over you.

I want to address a failed theory in men's ministry efforts to break the bondage of Porn. The motives are clear. We want men to be set free. However, every men's ministry effort I've known believes men must hold each other accountable to defeat Porn.

It simply does not work.

Men lie.

When I started speaking on authentic manhood and founded FivestarMan, I assumed that "holding men accountable" was a good option. The thinking is that we can confide in one another, confess our sins to one another, and encourage each other.

One man called me and said, "Neil, I have an addiction to Porn; I want you to hold me accountable."

After two phone calls, he ghosted me. He blocked my number. He unfriended me on Facebook. I used to preach for him once a year!

We are no longer friends. Not because I think less of him. Not because I think of his sin, which I don't. We're no longer friends because of what he told me; he is so ashamed of what I know he doesn't want to talk to me.

Every man who asked me to hold him accountable stopped taking my phone calls.

One problem with accountability is that it places one man in a dominating position over another. **God gave Man dominion over the Earth; He did not give Man domination over other men.**

> ***Domination:*** The exercise of control or influence over someone or something, or the state of being so controlled; submitted to the rule of another.

Domination is exercising power over another. It is not Biblical authority that flows through a protocol of leadership. I strongly encourage you to get my book, **Centurion Principle**, so that you can understand this vital distinction of leadership.

Jesus described domination as leadership that "lords" over others as the Gentiles did. It is satanic in nature. It is the seed of a perverted male-to-male relationship when one man submits to another man, not because of authority, but in a perverted relationship.

We have been taught the issue with men is we're not accountable. This theory subscribes to the notion that "shame" is a great motivator. The idea is if we enter into male-to-male relationships, we position ourselves to live the disciplined life of holiness by submission.

Men get together and say, "OK, we're going to hold one another accountable!"

Yet, it is very soon that the group fades into obscurity. Only a handful of men stay within the group. It is usually men who are very passive and play the victim.

Here are some obvious problems with this philosophy of men's ministry:

- Accountability positions men's leaders as judges. A man must live the righteousness of other men.
- Accountability positions the "*submitted*" as a child or even as a woman. It causes a grown man to be spoken down to.
- In attempting to implement this accountability strategy, many men's ministries have adopted militaristic themes and protocols as a strategy.
- When men are forced into this perversion of the peer-to-peer relationship, authentic manhood is weakened, emasculated, and effeminate.
- Every man who has ever asked me to hold him accountable eventually stopped talking to me.
- The suggestion is that somehow we need men to open their hearts and release their emotions in order to purify themselves.

Men are emotional; however, the emotions of men are directly related to their purposes.

Go to God!

Another fallacy of the accountability tactic is that it places a brother in the position of the Priest. So, rather than a man going to his High Priest of Confession, Jesus Christ, he goes to another man.

Your sins are not something that another man can claim! Only Christ can do that.

I have seen men try to dump their sins on other men, on their wives, and even on their children. They think spewing their sins on others is repentance. Don't do that. It's not fair for you to ask others to live your righteousness. Doing so is passivity!

You must be active in your repentance. Repentance is spiritual warfare.

Listen to me carefully and don't misunderstand or misapply what I am saying.

You must go to God to repent.

Going to a support group may encourage you and may, or may not, support you. But I know with all certainty that if you go to God, to your High Priest Jesus Christ, He will forgive you and empower you so that you're not obligated to sin.

Confession

> ***"Jesus, I come to you as my High Priest, Lord, and Savior. I confess my sins to you and you alone. Only you can cleanse me from my attraction to the bed of Ishtar. I will never allow lust to attract the attention of my eyes, nor will I surrender my manhood and the passion of my loins to her. I will not bed Ishtar again. I realize that I***

> ***have practiced idolatry, and I repent. Have mercy on me, O' Lord. Have mercy on me. In Jesus' Name. Amen."***

If accountability doesn't work. What do we do?

We walk in agreement.

> ***I also tell you this: If two of you agree here on earth concerning anything you ask, my Father in heaven will do it for you. —Matthew 18:19 (New Living Translation)***

> ***Can two people walk together without agreeing on the direction? —Amos 3:3***

I can't hold you accountable, but I can walk in agreement with you. Purpose gives you directional intent. That means that when you know WHY you are and WHO you are, you will also see WHERE you are going.

You have a destiny. I can agree with you about getting there.

If I call you to hold you accountable, my dialogue may sound like this...
"Hey, how are you doing? Did you live right this week? Did you look at Porn? Did you lust for anyone this week? Did you have your quiet time with God? Did you read the Bible? Come on, man, are you going to do this or not? What kind of man are you?"

If I call you to walk in agreement with you, it will sound like this...
"Hey, my friend. I prayed for you today. I have expectations

for you. I am expecting God to show Himself strong on your behalf. I know that you are strong enough and capable enough to resist anything that would come against you. No weapon forged against you will succeed. No, you're a champion! You're a righteous man! You walk in victory, and you will defeat your foe. You're going to prosper today. When you get home, your wife and children will celebrate you as the man of the home! Blessings! Be strong and be a man!"

If I called you with the accountability script, you would stop talking to me. I also know you will take my call every morning if I call you with the agreement script.

> ***Encourage one another daily, as long as it is called "Today," so that none of you may be hardened by sin's deceitfulness. —Hebrews 3:13 (New International Version)***

I wrote a 365-day devotional, what I call a daily word of encouragement, named **The Daily Champion.** It is free. We deliver it to tens of thousands of men daily. Sign up to receive it at TheDailyChampion.com.

You will be encouraged every morning with a 3-to-5-minute word of encouragement. Each day is written from the book of Proverbs. I hope to turn your daily commute into communion.

Each week, we have the **FivestarMan Champions Livestream** to engage with men across the Americas — North, Mexico, Central, and South America. We've launched FivestarMan Brazil to reach men daily and weekly with the message of authentic manhood.

So, you need someone to walk in agreement with you? We're here. That is why **FivestarMan.com** exists.

8

Destiny: Intended for the Heavens

> ***The first man, Adam, became a living soul.***
>
> ***The last Adam became the life-giving Spirit. However, the spiritual didn't come first. The natural precedes the spiritual. The first man was from the dust of the earth; the second Man is Yahweh, from the realm of heaven. The first one, made from dust, has a race of people just like him, who are also made from dust. The One sent from heaven has a race of heavenly people who are just like him. Once we carried the likeness of the man of dust, but now let us carry the likeness of the man of heaven. — 1 Corinthians 15:45-49 (The Passion Translation)***

Notice the scripture does not say the second Adam but the Last Adam. The Last Adam is Jesus Christ. As the Last Adam, Jesus began a new human species — a new man. This new man would be indwelt with the Holy Spirit.

So now, there are two types of humans —those who are of the natural and those of us who are of the supernatural. We are not merely human; now we are sons of God, born of the incorruptible Seed of God's Word.

Intended for the Heavens

There's a gravitational weight for Man to remain grounded on this Earth. Yet, there is also an adventurous spirit that propels men to reach.

To reach new heights, Man must become wiser and spiritually empowered. Man must become stronger. Man was not made for the Earth. The Earth was made for Man.

Once a man has tasted the heavenly gift, his walk on Earth becomes purposeful, passionate, and destined. Now is the time for Man to set his sights higher and become the Man intended for the heavens.

The Gravitational Decline of Humanity

You're aware things are getting worse. Sin has gravity. There is a weight to sin.

> ***Therefore, since we are surrounded by such a great cloud of witnesses, let us throw off everything that hinders and the sin that so easily entangles. —Hebrews 12:1 (New International Version)***

Sin entangles men. You get caught in a network of troubles. One thing leads to another. Soon, everything crumbles.

> ***For although they knew God, they neither glorified him as God nor gave thanks to him, but their thinking became futile and their foolish hearts were darkened. Although they claimed to be wise, they became fools and exchanged the glory of the immortal God for images made to look like mortal human beings and birds and animals and reptiles. — Romans 1:21-23 (New International Version)***

In the 1960s, things began to change in America. America began to rebel against the Judeo/Christian principles of our foundation.

The ethics, freedoms, and laws the United States of America was founded upon relate to the religious writings, beliefs, values, or traditions held in common by Judaism and Christianity.

Divorce laws were weakened. A few sympathetic circumstances led us to soften the restrictions on divorce. There was a time when you had to have a reason to divorce. Today, you don't need a reason.

Newly divorced and young singles began to cast off the restraints of the old boundary stones of relationships, and the sexual revolution erupted.

Along with the sexual revolution, infanticide (abortion) was legalized by the Supreme Court hearing a fraudulent case, *Roe V. Wade*.

Prayer was removed from public schools and, in most cases, the public squares.

The entertainment industry jumped on board and pushed the cultural norms to the edge of polite society.

Playboy and Hustler magazines brought high-gloss pornography to the shelves of bookstores, just above the reach of the average 12-year-old.

Homosexuality entered the scene first with humor. Same-sex couples began to demand equal rights for their partnerships. The decline reached the moment of decision, and the Supreme Court threw out precedent and removed the ancient boundary stone of marriage. The White House was flashed with rainbow colors celebrating the landmark decision.

Those orchestrating the radical transformation of our nation would not settle there. Within two weeks, a national retail chain opened its bathroom doors to transgender people. Of course, transgender people are not satisfied with their identity changes; they want much more abhorrent behavior — pedophilia.

> ***Therefore God gave them over in the sinful desires of their hearts to sexual impurity for the degrading of their bodies with one another. They exchanged the truth about God for a lie and worshiped and served created things rather than the Creator—who is forever praised. Amen.***
>
> ***Because of this, God gave them over to shameful lusts. Even their women exchanged natural sexual relations***

> ***for unnatural ones. In the same way, the men also abandoned natural relations with women and were inflamed with lust for one another. Men committed shameful acts with other men and received in themselves the due penalty for their error. —Romans 1:24-27 (New International Version)***

Paul perfectly describes the present culture. The decline of our nation is hitting rock bottom.

How will we live and flourish in our purposes in a culture of delusion and depravity? Now is the time for us to be wiser and Spiritually empowered. We must become stronger!

Wiser

> ***We do, however, speak a message of wisdom among the mature, but not the wisdom of this age or of the rulers of this age, who are coming to nothing. No, we declare God's wisdom, a mystery that has been hidden and that God destined for our glory before time began. None of the rulers of this age understood it, for if they had, they would not have crucified the Lord of glory. — 1 Corinthians 2:6-8 (New International Version)***

It's important to remember the rulers of this age do not understand the times in which we live. They act as if they are smart and cunning. They mock and ridicule, yet they are ignorant of their actions. They are destined for destruction.

> ***Then we will no longer be immature like children. We***

> ***won't be tossed and blown about by every wind of new teaching. We will not be influenced when people try to trick us with lies so clever they sound like the truth. — Ephesians 4:14 (New Living Translation)***

We are destined for glory. God holds secrets in storage for us. Now that we live in these times, we must become wiser in dealing with life. This is a time for mature men to step up and lead their families.

Seriously, you must become wiser.

"Knowledge makes a man unfit to be a slave." ~ Frederick Douglass

You can't live a passive, distracted, uncommitted life! You need wisdom.

When Solomon was given the throne of Israel following his father David's death, he desperately needed the wisdom to handle the affairs of God's people. There was an enormous amount of money in the treasury. There were leaders of the military maneuvering for positions. Siblings wanted the throne. Enemies wanted their land. It was a dangerous time for the transition of power and the anointing that came with it.

One night, the Lord appeared to Solomon and said, "Ask what I shall give you." (1 Kings 3:5 New International Version).

Solomon answered, "Give your servant, therefore, an understanding mind to govern your people, that I may discern between good and evil, for who is able to govern this your great people?" (verse 9).

The Lord was pleased with Solomon's response. Because Solomon showed wisdom to ask for wisdom, God granted him everything he did not request. Solomon received a wise and discerning heart, but he also received wealth, fame, victory over his enemies, and everything else you can imagine.

God is pleased when we ask for wisdom.

> ***If any of you lacks wisdom, you should ask God, who gives generously to all without finding fault, and it will be given to you. But when you ask, you must believe and not doubt, because the one who doubts is like a wave of the sea, blown and tossed by the wind. That person should not expect to receive anything from the Lord. Such a person is double-minded and unstable in all they do. —James 1:5-8 (New International Version)***

You may not inherit a throne to govern, yet you still need the wisdom to manage your household. You may not have a trillion dollar treasury, yet you still need the wisdom to manage your personal economy. You may not have siblings rivaling you, yet you still need the wisdom to flourish in relationships.

What I do know is that you certainly have spiritual enemies. You need the wisdom of God to defeat them.

Please listen to me. You must be wise every day. You can't take a break for a moment.

> ***Live no longer as the Gentiles do, for they are hopelessly confused. Their minds are full of darkness; they wander far from the life God gives because they have closed their minds and hardened their hearts against him. They have no sense of shame. They live for lustful pleasure and eagerly practice every kind of impurity. —Ephesians 4:17–19 (New Living Translation)***

I wrote TheDailyChampion.com to provide a daily word of encouragement. I strongly recommend you sign up to have them sent to you each morning.

Pray this Prayer

"Father, you said that if I lack wisdom, you would be generous to me. You do not qualify me; you simply give wisdom because I asked. I desperately need wisdom to navigate my life. I need wisdom to be a husband. I need wisdom to father my children. I need wisdom for my finances. I need wisdom to position my family to live in faith. I need wisdom to protect myself from the seductive spirit of Ishtar. Please, Lord, give me the wisdom I need as a man. In Jesus' Name, Amen."

Spirit-Empowered

> ***But you, my friends, constantly and progressively build yourselves up on the foundation of your most holy faith by praying every moment in the Spirit. Fasten your hearts to the love of God and receive the mercy of our Lord Jesus Christ, who gives us eternal life. —Jude 1:20 (The Passion Translation)***

When you pray in the Spirit, you strengthen yourself.

The phrase "praying every moment in the Spirit" references to the strengthening and enlightening experience the Holy (Authorized) Spirit gives us. Even when we don't know what to pray for or about, the Holy (Authorized) Spirit prays through us.

> ***And in a similar way, the Holy Spirit takes hold of us in our human frailty to empower us in our weakness. For example, at times we don't even know how to pray or know the best things to ask for. But the Holy Spirit rises up within us to intercede for us. —Romans 8:26 (The Passion Translation)***

Rather than mingle with the evil spirit of Ishtar, communing with her in her filth, we have the opportunity for the Holy (Authorized) Spirit to commune with us, praying through us, interceding on our behalf.

There have been times when I was so desperate in spiritual warfare, knowing I was interceding between Heaven's will and Earth's frustration, all I could do was groan. I didn't have the words!

Yet, my groaning was Spiritual whispers doing warfare.

Listen, when you're facing troubles of many kinds, you need wisdom. You also need the Spirit-empowerment to come alongside you. These Holy Spirit groans and spiritual languages help shape our destiny.

For more information on Spirit Empowerment, we have a video teaching entitled **FUEL: The Spirit-Empowered Man** (https://championu.life/p/fuel)

Pray for Spirit Empowerment

> ***"Father, Jesus promised you would give me the Gift of the Holy Spirit. I am asking in faith that you would keep your promise. I know that you're not a man, that you can lie. I also know that you would make a promise with an expiration date. So, as a Believer in your Son, Jesus Christ, I ask that you Baptize me with the Holy Spirit so that I can receive power and the ability to pray in the Holy Spirit. In Jesus' Name, Amen."***

Stronger

> ***"I am about to go the way of all the earth," he said. "So be strong, act like a man. Observe what the Lord your God requires: Walk in obedience to him, and keep his decrees and commands, his laws and regulations, as written in the Law of Moses. Do this so that you may prosper in all you do and wherever you go and that the Lord may keep his promise to me: 'If your descendants watch how they live, and if they walk faithfully before me with all their heart and soul, you will never fail to have a successor on the throne of Israel.' —1 Kings 2:2-4 (New International Version)***

That was David's charge to his son, Solomon. Of all the things he could have said as he lay dying, David's charge to his son is,

"Be strong, act like a man."

I want to charge you, **"Be strong, act like a man."**

It's time to get stronger in mind, body, and spirit.

> ***Do not conform to the pattern of this world, but be transformed by the renewing of your mind. Then you will be able to test and approve what God's will is—his good, pleasing and perfect will. —Romans 12:2 (New International Version)***

This portion of the book may seem out of place for the subject. However, I have seen that men who keep up their pursuit of manliness — authentic manhood — also have a strong sense of honor that disciplines them.

Mind

Read the Word of God

- Create a discipline of reading one chapter of Proverbs every day of the month. There are 31 chapters. Champions do daily what the average man does occasionally.
- Read through the Bible in a year. I created this daily discipline years ago; then, I read through the Bible every 90-days. It only takes about 30-minutes a day.

Read One Non-Fiction Book a Month

- The average millionaire reads one non-fiction book a month.

The average American reads one book a year.
- Reading requires incredible energy because your brain uses power to process. I started by reading in 15-minute bursts. I focus for 15-minutes then I move around and do something for a minute or two. Then I go back to reading.
- When I am traveling, I am listening to either the Bible or a book.

Avoid Too Much News

- I used to be a news junkie. I have withdrawn from having the news on. I no longer need it.
- I still get the news but I only find the highlights of current events. I do not get sucked into the drama and talking heads.

Having Meaningful Conversations

- Do not gossip.
- Do not slander.
- Avoid godless chatter.
- Don't get entangled in worthless arguments on social media. Because of what I do with the message of authentic manhood, I attract all types of hate speech, mockery, and foolery on social media. I have to be careful to avoid getting distracted by them.

Be a Life-long Learner

- Don't think that you know it all.
- Constantly learn new skills.
- Keep your mind active. I try to keep my mind sharp by not

using the calculator for math problems. I play word games with my family.

Body

Do you not know that in a race all the runners run, but only one gets the prize? Run in such a way as to get the prize. —1 Corinthians 9:24 (New International Version)

Eat to Fuel

- Don't make food your comforter.
- Feast on holidays. Fast in times of trial.
- As I have gotten older, I realized that I must condition my body to finish my race.
- Eat meat. You need protein.
- Make sure you maintain testosterone levels.
- Have a good multivitamin.

Exercise

- Keep moving.
- You don't have to be a gym rat.
- Have a moderate exercise plan that works for you.

Grooming

- Keep your clothes clean and pressed.
- Stay up to date in classical style.
- Frequent a good barber.
- Keep your shoes or boots shined.

- Don't be sloppy.
- Keep your fingernails trimmed.
- Have ear hairs, nose hairs, and eyebrows trimmed.
- Keep your teeth maintained.

Physician

- Have a yearly checkup.
- Don't fear sickness. Fear of sickness is often worse than any virus there is. Don't buy into it.

Spirit

My mission is to live proficiently in faith, love, health, and prosperity.

Faith

- I read the Word of God because faith comes from hearing the Word.
- I confess the Word of God openly and out loud.
- I claim the promises of God as they are mine.
- I resist the spirit of fear and timidity.

Love

- I love God, my Savior Jesus Christ.
- I love my wife.
- I love my children and grandchildren.
- I love my friends.
- I love my enemies — those who are spiteful and hateful.

I speak blessing over them. I don't war against flesh and blood.

Health

- I work to maintain a healthy lifestyle.
- I don't drink sodas or alcohol.
- I am working to be trim, fit, lean, and strong.

Prosperity

- Prosperity means I have what I need financially to fulfill my purpose.
- To do so, I must have cash flow.
- I work to have multiple streams of income.
- I am not a wage slave. I am entrepreneurial.
- I do not horde. I am a giver.

I've included my list of what I am doing to be stronger because so many men need to step up their games. I hope my list is an encouragement to you.

9

Conclusion

My friend, I have spoken as clearly as I could regarding the spirit of Porn, namely the evil spirit Ishtar. I weep when I hear of men she has seduced. She is evil. She is filthy. She hates you.

I pray for you. I really do.

I want what is best for you. I do what I do — write, speak, and teach men because I've seen the destruction of so many lives. You're worth so much more than to be brought down by the Harlot, Ishtar.

Say out loud, **"I will not bed Ishtar."**
Repeat it louder, **"I will NOT bed Ishtar."**
One more time, like a man, **"I WILL NOT BED ISHTAR!"**

Finally,
Be Strong and Act Like a Man!

Printed in the USA
CPSIA information can be obtained
at www.ICGtesting.com
JSHW010011280723
45456JS00006B/322

9 798218 107529